LEADERSHIP IS NOT A BOWLER HAT

LEADERSHIP IS NOT A BOWLER HAT

PETER J. PRIOR

David & Charles
Newton Abbot London North Pomfret (Vt) Vancouver

'There is more than opportunity for leadership now, there is stark necessity for it. Men are ripe for intelligent, understanding, personal leadership, they would rather be led than managed.'

Field Marshal Slim

ISBN 0 7153 7487 7
Library of Congress Catalog Card Number 77–89373
© 1977 Peter J. Prior

Set in 11 on 12pt Baskerville
and printed in Great Britain
by Redwood Burn Limited
for David & Charles (Publishers) Limited
Brunel House   Newton Abbot ▪ Devon

Published in the United States of America
by David & Charles Inc
North Pomfret   Vermont 05053   USA

Published in Canada
by Douglas David & Charles Limited
1875 Welch Street   North Vancouver   BC

CONTENTS

PREFACE

This book promotes the following idea:

To arrest our national economic decline we need to produce more at lower cost. So far we have tried to do this mainly by the techniques of what is broadly called 'scientific management'.

Whilst these techniques may help, they are not the final factor. Personal leadership is vital to their successful use and, today, is the most significant motivating factor which remains available to managers.

A firm belief in the solid value of personal leadership must be revived if we are to survive the present crisis, but—

'Leadership is not a bowler hat ...'

1

A CHALLENGE—AND AN OPPORTUNITY

I came to my present employers, a firm of cider-makers, from the aluminium industry and, shortly after joining, I observed to a farmer who supplied us with apples that a particular tree had no apples on it.

'No, it doesn't', he agreed, 'and we didn't get any from it last year.' Armed with the confidence that an apple tree was no different from a machine, I asked him, 'If it doesn't produce apples, why keep it?'

The farmer paused for a moment and then said, 'Well there's a special reason in this case—it's a pear tree.'

Fortunately, perhaps, this book is not concerned with such technical matters, but confines itself, quite simply, to the question of Britain's survival as a country fit to live in, and the present state of our economy and the threat this poses to the nation's destiny. I still cannot tell an apple tree from a pear tree, but let us hope this won't matter.

In the course of time, some latter-day Gibbon will almost certainly record for posterity the decline and fall of the British Empire. It is to be hoped that he will not be able to include also, in such a treatise, the decline and fall of the United Kingdom economy, but, at present, the grounds for such a hope do not seem promising. Shrouded as they are in a fog of complexity, Britain's economic problems are not easy to identify, to analyse, or to solve.

It may be possible to simplify the position by agreeing that most of our present problems stem from the low rate of growth of the gross national product—the goods and the services which we as a population produce. In the final analysis, it is our failure, in recent decades, to increase our total national output at a sufficient rate which is at the root of all our present economic ills.

As recently as the late 1950s, a valid consensus of opinion existed which believed that things were on the up-and-up and that the whole standard of life in these islands was progressively improving. 'You've never had it so good', Mr Macmillan told the nation. The redistribution of wealth had improved the lot of the less fortunate, but, to a much greater extent, a steady increase in the gross national product had apparently improved the lot of everyone.

Since the end of the seller's market in the early 1960s, however, and especially today, no such consensus of opinion has prevailed. If there has been any agreement among every section of the population since the advent of rampant inflation, it has been that things are getting worse; worse for everybody except, possibly, for the small parasitical element which contrives, with some success, to live off the backs of us all. In recent years, the rate of increased consumption has not been matched by increased production, with the result that, as the redistribution of wealth continues apace, the satisfaction of those who have gained has been outpaced by the dissatisfaction of those who have lost.

By any standards, and especially by comparison with most other industrial nations, we have, for a number of years, experienced an economic decline which successive governments have failed to arrest. There are many detailed causes of this decline, but, when it comes to the crunch, the most significant factor of all is that increases in national output have singularly failed to match the needs of the population's insistent urge to consume.

In the interests of simplicity, throughout this book I write of increasing our output in terms of the manufacturing industry, although the principles stated are in no way confined to this area of our national effort. The need for more effective work is as vital in government, the public services, the armed forces and the nationalised industries, as it is in private enterprise.

In the following pages I have attempted to restate our problem and to outline a means of solving it by reducing the matter to simpler and more easily definable issues with which we can all get to grips. The fixing of objectives, decision-making, achievement and, above all, the inspired use of personal leadership is the stuff of this book; such leadership is universally applicable and is, at the moment, universally needed.

For those who do not accept the basic premise that what matters is increased national output—often called 'productivity', I shall try, briefly, to justify it, but not at such length as to depart from my main subject. Wittingly or unwittingly, many industrial units are, in one way or another, contributing to Britain's current decline, but it must also be said that there are, of course, an encouraging number of honourable exceptions and to these one must not preach. Nevertheless, this book is addressed to managers in general and, particularly, to top managers, because effective reform can come only from the top. It is brief in the hope that significant leaders of industry and the public service will somehow find time to read it. Many may see it as a restatement of the obvious, but, even so, it may serve a useful purpose for those who already think in this way, by providing a bridge to help them extend their thinking to others.

Britain's present situation offers far greater opportunity for change than has existed for many decades past and the present moment is, therefore, the critical time to speak out. People are not inherently resistant to change; in some areas they may resist, but in many others they will respond, given the right leadership. At present the whole nation is suffering from a feeling of common adversity, coupled with the growing realisation that we are all in the same boat. We are now less divided by political slogans since political slogans have become totally discredited, as, fortunately, have many of our less realistic politicians.

The need to tackle the common problem offers at least the prospective benefit of a common agreement. It is easier to mobilise concerted action when the nature and origin of our economic problems are more generally accepted. Today, the 55 million crew members of the British ship of State have a much clearer sight of the rocks which threaten the voyage. If a promised land can be shown with the same simple clarity, then perhaps we can be persuaded to work together and pull in the same direction for our mutual salvation.

It is true, of course, that the need to increase productivity in order to arrest our economic decline has been greatly accentuated by the change in our national environment. For a century or more, the existence of an empire enabled us to live more easily from the benefits which it bestowed upon us. Moreover, the loss of our ability to exploit overseas possessions has been aggravated by the simultaneous increase in competition from emergent industrial nations and, more recently, from the Common Market. As self-sufficiency is promoted elsewhere, so our need to develop our home resources has increased at the very time when we are less inclined to tackle the problem.

> *'The trouble with the British is that they never see the writing on the wall until they have their backs to it.'*
>
> *Leigh Hunt*

For years we have been much too complacent and only now, when the harsh realities of our economic position stand out in stark relief, has recognition of the need for reform become more generally accepted. Change is in the air because, in a desperate situation, change has a more than equal chance of bringing salvation. Now that the passive acceptance of our problems is being rejected, can we not reach a common agreement on the necessary remedies?

McKinsey & Co, the respected American management consultants, have recently published the booklet, *The Investment Challenge*, which served a very useful purpose in demonstrating with commendable clarity and with a brevity which I would like to emulate, the inevitable and circular inter-dependence of the nation's present economic ailments.

Using the McKinsey circle, I choose to start at the factor of 'poor productivity' and, in the interests of telegraphic communication, I hope the reader will accept the consequences to which this factor leads. In the McKinsey circle poor productivity leads to rising wage costs, to declining profits and to low investment, thus to low industrial growth, fewer jobs, bad industrial relations and thus back to poor productivity. Lost jobs provoke other problems as well, such as rising public expenditure, higher taxes, high cost

10

capital and low investment and inflation, but these are separate questions.

In this vicious circle, in which the British economy finds itself, remedial measures may be needed at all points in the circle, but the major breakthrough to rectify the nation's economic decline is only likely to be achieved through a determined effort to produce more for the same cost. Most reforms require government action, but this is one which is within the power of each company, each executive and each public servant to influence.

One of the most puzzling factors about our present national situation is why so many should believe, so blindly, that a mere reshuffling of the cards in the national pack can give the majority of the players a better hand than they held before. That the majority can *have* more, when the majority is not *producing* more, is so simple a fallacy as to be plainly absurd. Mercifully, such respected trades union leaders as Jack Jones, Len Murray and others are, at the time of writing, helping to bring this point home to all.

This particular lead in a new national thought process has come from what, to many, may seem an unexpected quarter, but, for-tunately, it has come from a quarter that has major influence and at the time it is most needed. The Trades Union Congress has recently emerged as a body which is giving a strong national lead in changing the approach to the sharing of the national cake. For this reason alone, now is the time for government, industry and management, to rethink their whole approach to what, at last, has become 'the common cause'—higher productivity for our very national survival.

I believe it is by a new emphasis on personal leadership at all levels that we can find the answer.

2
GOVERNMENT INTERVENTION IN BUSINESS

Our prime concern should be with ways of increasing the total size of the national cake by greater productivity, and not with the continuation of our present futile squabbling about how the national cake, whether it be large or small, should be divided. It is with this division, however, that government seems mainly to concern itself and, in consequence, we must take into account the increasing degree of political intervention in the affairs of industry. Day by day the interface between Government and industry becomes ever more complex and the scope for businessmen to make objective decisions becomes less and less.

The desirability of government intervention is often justified by the bland assumption that the advantages claimed for it will actually materialise. Quite often they do not and frequently the very opposite outcome results. Indeed some industries capable of distinctive achievement are precluded from it by the well intentioned but ill conceived interventions of government or of its officials, many of whom change their jobs too frequently to acquire an appreciation of the relevant factors.

The electricity industry is a case in point: inevitably a complex management entity, it has for years been the victim of intervention and experiment, of vacillation and deferred decisions. Under what in practice amount to the restrictive ministrations of the Treasury, the Department of Energy, and NEDO, the industry may now have to contend with the outcome provoked by the NEDO, Bullock and Plowden Reports. Although the proposed Energy Commission may appear to be a beneficial development, in practice it is likely to provide yet another layer of control. All things con-

> *'You cannot bring about prosperity by discouraging thrift. You cannot strengthen the weak by weakening the strong. You cannot help the wage-earner by pulling down the wage-payer. You cannot help the poor by destroying the rich. You cannot establish sound security on borrowed money. You cannot keep out of trouble by spending more than you earn. You cannot build character and courage by taking away a man's initiative and independence. You cannot help men permanently by doing for them what they should be doing for themselves.'*
>
> *Abraham Lincoln*

sidered, the industry has not shown up too badly. Its executives have been strong enough to adopt what might be called the 'lifeboat' philosophy under which there is an inflexible determination to survive as a team in a corporate lifeboat despite troubled waters, hostile elements and defective charts.

It is difficult to identify many areas where the intervention has, on balance, been beneficial to the economy as a whole, since so much of it has been motivated by direct considerations of division whilst little more than lip service has been paid to the vital need to increase total national output.

Many politicians and trades unionists still insist upon regarding the ownership of industry as a vital current issue whereas, in reality, ownership is now of less importance. Fewer shares are in the hands of private individuals today, so that institutional investors, including employees' pension funds, are now highly significant. This wider spread of ownership may be much more accountable and, in the long run, may produce better results than the almost unaccountable public ownership of industry which has grown apace with recent legislation.

The justification for nationalisation by the Left is based on arguments which may have been applicable many years ago, but which are mainly irrelevant now. The days of the exploiting mineowners and downtrodden workers have long since vanished, and to demand public ownership on this sort of premise is no more sensible than to justify it on the vague and insupportable assertion that bigger is bound to be better. From recent experience there is very little evidence to support the contention that public ownership is, on principle, beneficial to society. On the other

13

hand, there is some evidence to indicate that the obstruction of leadership and decisive management which it involves has, at times, encouraged the decline of an industry, rather than its development.

A few large privately owned companies still do exist and it is possible that some of these may be less progressive than they should be in the field of industrial relations. However, such companies are the exception rather than the rule. Inefficiency is more often the characteristic of any large organisation, rather than only of those which are publicly owned and with which, it seems, the Conservative Party invariably equates it.

Ownership does still carry one 'right' which is highly relevant, however, but which is overdue for reform. This is the practice under which the owners of a company's shares are solely responsible for the appointment of that company's directors. It is illogical that the entire board of a company should be composed of the nominees of those who have invested their capital in it. Employees have done more than invest their money in the company, they have invested their lives in it, and it is quite inequitable that they should have no official say in the management of their own affairs.

In this respect, businessmen could have taken an initiative to put their own house in order and they will be at least partly to blame if new provisions for the appointment of directors are foisted on them by Government. Present company legislation certainly does not encourage the liberalisation of the director-appointing process and, even if it did, an instinctively authoritarian tradition still motivates many top industrialists. There remain, also, many easy arguments which can be called upon to veto the appointment of shopfloor directors, or to impede any similar extension of industrial democracy.

It is ironic that in Britain, which lays claim to having the longest record of political freedom and democracy, we should still be so far behind such countries as Germany and France in our acceptance of these liberalising concepts of management. However, it is now a little late for scaffold repentance in these matters, since Government direction on the appointment of directors seems imminent and many businessmen are resigned to waiting helplessly for what they see as a further erosion of their rightful authority.

As it is highly relevant to the development of team spirit within a

firm, it is worth noting, however, that the idea of shopfloor directors in the board room is being reasonably well accepted by many
businessmen, subject to one proviso. In these instances the
reaction is most often: 'As long as the worker directors are our own
people, appointed by our own people, we shan't worry'. But,
bearing in mind that governments often dance to the tune of the
Left, many industrialists fear that nominations to the board will
come from trades union headquarters and may be of officials not
actually employed by, or concerned with, the business.

For my own part, I must admit to the belief that the increasing
intervention of Government in the control of industry has been the
most significant factor in our present economic decline. The im-
position of progressively more involved restrictions has had a
mollycoddling effect against the impact of personal economic
hazard. Measures such as the 'Pay Freeze' have developed a
situation where the industrious are lumped together with the idle,
and have prohibited the just reward of those responsible for
increased productivity. In such a situation, where man's initiative
and natural desire to be effective are stifled by restrictive
legislation, the need for good leadership is heavily underlined.
Leaders must now motivate their teams on a diet of praise and encouragement, rather than money rewards.

In consequence, the current preoccupation with 'participation'
is highly relevant, although it is not for this reason that the principle is being promoted. Good firms, which have worked to achieve
harmonious industrial relations in the past, already involve their
employees in the company's problems and decisions, but involv-
ing them formally has been difficult because of the limitations of
current company legislation. It is a pity that the progressive companies could not be permitted to continue with whatever style of
participative management they have found to be workable, but
will be obliged to suffer under new Government directions which
may, in the event, do more harm than good.

Participation by employee workers in the management of the
organisation which employs them must come. Participation is essential to the development of team achievement. It is vital, if the
catalytic effect of personal leadership is to ensure that team effort
leads to achievement.

3
A POSITIVE ROLE FOR THE UNIONS

Loyalty and toleration are, generally, uneasy bedfellows. Most of us tend to adopt, in our industrial lives, the attitudes of blind loyalty which are more typical of football team supporters. There is no harm in supporting a team provided that its true constituents have been correctly identified. Industry might learn the lesson that few football clubs would reach the First Division if ten of the players were always at loggerheads with their captain, or, for that matter, with their manager. All teams start at the top.

Participation is about team building and it is not only company owners and company managers whose approach is at fault. Whilst there are extremist advocates of authoritarian management, they are, unfortunately, matched on the union side by an equally vociferous minority of Left-wing extremists—advocates of antagonism rather than of co-operation.

The philosophies of either side are more likely to lead to company collapse, than to company success.

The virtues of competition and the virtues of industrial democracy are often extolled, but rarely defined. In the field of international affairs, the slogan 'My country, right or wrong' fell into discredit at the turn of the century and was finally buried during World War II. In politics unfortunately, 'My Party, right or wrong' still prevails, at least among politicians who, in some extraordinary way, seem to remain in blissful ignorance of the average British voter's disillusion with their outdated attitudes. 'What is the policy of your party to rectify this problem?', asks the TV interviewer, almost always in vain. Constructive replies from the spokesmen of either party are the exception rather than the rule. Instead with boring regularity comes the inevitable reply, 'It's the fault of the other side.'

There is some evidence that, in industry, the responses are now more mature, more constructive, that progress has been made. The traditional attitudes of antagonism between management and the unions have been eliminated in many small firms and, even in large ones, where the problems are so much more difficult, new and more tolerant policies are taking root. The instinctive reaction of 'My side, right or wrong' must be totally eliminated, however, if real progress is to be made in the revival of the national economy.

The growing realisation that the prosperity, happiness and security of shopfloor workers, as well as of managers, is linked with the success of the company which employs them, is the seed now being sown by progressive trade unionists. This seed may well fall on fertile ground for, in truth, 95 per cent of the British population are moderates by inclination. In our heart of hearts we know that toleration and co-operation are the only true roads to achievement and thus to prosperity.

Moderate policies are never easy to present, however. They always seem less colourful, less distinctive, and are certainly less emotive than those promoted by the extremists of either side; but the extremists, at best, constitute only the remaining 5 per cent of the population. If some managers feel that the rank and file trade unionist is sometimes being led by the nose by extremists of the Left, then managers must take even greater care to ensure that they are not themselves misled by extremists of the Right.

There may be a few wild men of the extreme Left who sincerely believe the total break up of present society is a necessary pre-liminary to their proletarian millenium, but their numbers are few and are diminishing. The forces of moderation at last show signs that they are prepared to assert, with energy, a policy of tolerant and progressive industrial reform. If my estimate that 95 per cent of the population are moderates is correct, then the new role of the union movement in harnessing moderation to our future prosperity could be, in the end, the most significant factor in our national recovery.

Participation is not just about power, it is about achievement through co-operation. The use of power without responsibility in the control of industry will be no advantage to national prosperity. It will amount to a criminal betrayal of the trust which workers are entitled to place in their leaders. In the old days of positive confrontation, of mineowner versus miner, the defence of workers' rights was probably the only solution, even to the last ditch, but now most unionists recognise that the philosophies of antagonism are irrelevant in today's environment—as dead as the dodo.

Union objectives must be updated, not only on a broad national basis, but also at the local level. Union activities should everywhere act as a lubricant to co-operation not as an abrasive; as a spur to participation for the common good. A union leader said to me recently, 'We must have conflict or we wouldn't have our members' subscriptions.' If many others have this feeling then the question which they should ask themselves is this: 'Conflict with whom?' There are surely sufficient real enemies lurking in the surrounding industrial undergrowth without looking for enemies within the camp itself.

Nor must managers, if they claim to be leaders, shirk their ultimate responsibility, since there is truth in Montgomery's belief that there is no such thing as a bad soldier, only bad officers. There is no doubt that the main initiative for the improvement in industrial relations must come from the side of management, but the authority of the union movement as a whole, with huge forces at its disposal, will be greatly enhanced if unions reach out with initiatives of their own.

Such an initiative could be one of great promise since, in my experience, new approaches from unexpected quarters often prove to be the most effective ones. The element of surprise has won many a battle. Once offered, I believe that the response to union initiative in the field of participation would be more than proportional from the management side, but, what is more, the reputation of the whole union movement in the nation would be enormously enhanced. After all, it is in accordance with the commonest of sense for unionists to take up publicly the cause of greater productivity, a cause which lines the pockets of the main body of the workforce far more than it may incidentally line the pockets of managers or shareholders.

Unions today have a far greater opportunity than ever before to bridge the gap between management and men, to insist from their side that common corporate objectives, designed to achieve company success, are identified. The unions are in a far better position than anybody else to spell out the simple truth to everybody, that wealth must first be created before it can be divided.

This is the new challenge of the labour movement and it is a challenge which a new and progressive generation of trades union leaders are rapidly taking up. Let us hope that politicians, still obsessed by the sterile squabbles of yesteryear, will soon have the sense to follow their example.

4

TODAY'S INCENTIVE TO ACHIEVEMENT

Reversing our economic decline through greater productivity means, quite simply, that each of us must produce more from the same resources. More investment would certainly enhance such improvement, but that is a separate question. Some companies, and a few public bodies, have already shown that greater production from the same resources can be achieved and that this is a realistic objective, but they are the exception rather than the rule.

Increased productivity by every one of us is the only sure means by which we will break out of the vicious circle of decline, the means by which we will beat inflation, raise our exports to balance our overseas payments, improve our standard of living and, if the truth be known, satisfy those personal aspirations in which so many find they are deeply frustrated at present.

The time for legislative tinkering with the economic machine has passed. A vigorous and revolutionary new approach is now essential and it is my purpose to show that, not only is such a new approach possible, but that it would have universal national appeal and could be grasped by all groups in society with enthusiasm because of its clarity and its humanity.

It is a people approach, not a 'thing' approach and it is essentially simple. For years we have allowed ourselves to be persuaded by technocrats that our problems could be solved only by complex means or by pseudo-scientific methods. But our problems are now so basic, and show so little response to the convoluted manipulations of the theory-mongers, that we must return with all haste to first principles. Our problems will be solved only by the identification of common objectives and by the exercise of personal leadership in building up the people-teams necessary to attain them.

Three factors have changed recently in British industry and 'scientific management' has been mainly concerned with two of them: namely, the increased size of the average business, and its much more complex technology. These factors are susceptible to the scientific approach, but it is the implications of change in the third factor which remain largely unresolved and with which we are concerned. Since the advent of the Welfare State, and the disappearance of fear and poverty as social sanctions, compulsion, as an incentive to the attainment of industrial objectives, has largely disappeared. In many instances, nothing has replaced it and, in consequence, there exists today a motivational vacuum.

If productivity is to rise, this vacuum must be filled with a new incentive to achievement, a new motivational factor. We must recognise that compulsion through fear, as a means of achieving results, is no longer on. We have to find a new factor with which people can relate, voluntarily and willingly.

There are two main reasons why people do things: either because they are forced to, or because they derive pleasure and satisfaction from achievement. Thus, the only substitute for compulsion is inclination—the inclination of an individual, and of society in general, to achieve agreed objectives through working as a team. Few would argue that teamwork cannot achieve economic miracles when it is inspired by good personal leadership.

'Field Marshal Allenby never quite realised that men are governed through the emotions rather than through the intelligence.'

General Wavell

This assertion should not be taken as a total indictment of scientific management which has made, and will make in the future, vital contributions to solving the problems inherent in any large enterprise or new technology. Scientific management is concerned with reason rather than with emotion; it is concerned with logic and with things rather than people. Indeed, in the field of personal motivation, it is extremely likely that scientific management has created more problems than it has solved.

Personnel officers may claim to have approached the problems of the individual through social science, but the present state of human and industrial relations, in many critical areas of British business, says little for the success of their efforts. Personnel departments work generally 'by the book', they follow devoutly the teachings of their gurus and speak rarely in terms of individual personal leadership. Indeed, until recently, the very word 'leadership' was regarded at many levels of management with suspicion; the word had militaristic undertones, or implied the notion of two classes of people—the leaders and those who were led, sometimes even by the nose. It was, regrettably, a word which had little appeal to the industrialist, the manager, the trade unionist or the public servant.

If leadership, as a quality, is the factor which could enable us to break out of the vicious circle of economic decline, then we must grasp it. We must identify and harness this personal quality; we must modify our reactions to it and, henceforward, employ it un-selfconsciously, with imagination and determination, to develop the latent resources of the British people.

5

MANAGEMENT SCIENCE—
ONLY A TOOL

In the handling of human relationships, relatively small personal initiatives often promote a more than proportionate response, and it is with such initiatives that leadership is concerned. When relatively minor disputes provoke the instinctively aggressive postures which bring production to a juddering halt in the big firm, it is the bold human initiative, the warm touch of personal leadership which will evoke a responsive reaction when reasonable argument gets nowhere. The blood, toil, tears and sweat which Winston Churchill promised if the war was to be won was an emotive approach, but it had real human appeal and drew the response which led to ultimate victory.

Many responsible business people are now reaching the conclusion that a touch more leadership and a little less science may well be the solution to our present problems. But what is the scope in industry today for the exercise of personal leadership? In some firms the only current manifestation of this 'personal quality' comes from the strike organiser at the factory gate whose cry of 'All out' is met by an immediate and total response which must curl the toes of many of our managers with envy. Why should the atmosphere of the average large firm not be made more conducive to the exercise of leadership from other quarters? With a greater or lesser expectation of success, according to his personal merit, why, then, should the exceptional company chairman not mount his own soapbox at the works' gate and cry 'All in'? Why not, indeed? Is it tradition, or fear of non-conformity which forbids such a direct appeal?

Regrettably, it is all too often the case in big organisations, both industrial and public, that the sheer size and complexity of the organisation structure leaves no scope at all for personal leadership to be exercised, except by the one, often remote, man at the very top. Executives have neither distinct enough objectives, nor adequate delegated authority, to promote a situation under which such leadership qualities as they may possess can be properly utilised. Should a manager be sufficiently rash to take any firm leadership initiative, the full wrath of the functional experts, the personnel managers and the accountants, will descend upon him. The dedicated management scientists will declare that the manager has 'upset the consultative procedures', 'short-circuited the channels of communication', or committed that cardinal sin of 'setting a precedent'.

> *'At the risk of being lynched, I would say that anybody who has a Personnel Department mismanages people . . .'*
>
> *Peter Drucker*

This all-pervasive horror of precedent setting is the sure-fire means by which technocrats smother at birth the constructive initiatives of potential leaders which, given free rein, could threaten the alleged supremacy of the laboratory-nurtured, clinically sterile, jargon-wrapped, techniques-for-all-occasions brigade. These blinkered technocrats must be persuaded that the setting of precedents is exactly what leadership is all about. The true and justified role of management science is to ensure that a management environment exists in which personal leadership can freely operate. And that is the technocrats' role, full stop. In such situations the valid virtue of the management sciences can be properly exploited. The basic function of budgetary control, for example, is certainly not to restrict executive liberty, but to quantify it so that, by defining areas of authority in terms of the common factor of finance, one can encourage executives to operate with freedom, initiative and enthusiasm.

Management science must resolve the problems involved in breaking down the clear-cut objectives of top management into sub-objectives which can be clearly understood by each department of the business. It must promote the establishment of organisation structures which are direct and unambiguous and which permit free scope for individual initiative. Finally, management science must define responsibilities and encourage a genuine delegation of authority. Only when it has fulfilled these roles—its true roles—can the personal qualities of individual executives be harnessed to the achievement of the organisation's social and corporate objectives; only then can teams be built up through personal leadership to achieve positive results.

6
BREAKING DOWN THE BARRIERS

Replacement of the divisive attitudes and antagonistic postures which prevail in many large firms, by a new corporate team spirit which will fill the present motivational vacuum is more difficult to achieve in Britain than elsewhere. 'Class' identity reaches back over many, many years; each class has its particular beliefs and its different realities. The one thing they share is a host of poorly tested assumptions about each other. Centuries of freedom from vigorous political upheaval have also left us with an arthritic political environment. The instinctive resistance to change which is characteristic of British industry is due, as much as anything else, to a perpetuation of the class divisions which have for long seemed so natural a factor in our society.

It may well be true to suggest that the class divisions of yesteryear have disappeared, but, unfortunately, they have been replaced by others. Gone, perhaps, are the squires and the peasants, the officers and other-ranks, the gentlemen and the players, but somehow we have been left with this totally unnecessary and completely unreasonable industrial split—the division between management and men.

An instinctive belief that one section of society has a divine right to authority is a leftover from earlier class assumptions which, unfortunately, still finds acceptance by many top managers. If they cannot rethink their attitudes before the floodtide of 'progressive' legislation makes these attitudes totally irrelevant, then their companies may well follow the way of so many, once proud, British firms which have gone to the wall through their sheer inability to move with a changing environment.

In society, and in firms, each class has its different realities. Stable lads striking at Ascot 1975. (*Popperfoto*)

All the scientific management techniques in the world will not overcome this awesome obstacle to harmonious industrial relations, this unnecessary and anachronistic division between board room and shopfloor. Failure to recognise the division between management and men as the overriding obstacle to industrial progress is not, however, a failing of top management alone. Few politicians refer to it overtly, preferring to confine themselves to the less significant, but more emotive considerations of ownership which are so deeply rooted in the philosophies of either party. Fortunately, the TUC has probably done a great deal in recent months to expose the dangers which a continuance of this divided posture may bring.

Before effective teams can be created which can, through increased productivity, reverse our present decline, personal leadership has, firstly, to dissolve the artificially divided environment by breaking down the barriers and replacing them with trust.

A later chapter illustrates how management science can be used to develop a structure within which real leadership *can* operate, but this basic barrier to progress, this division in British

27

industry, must first be faced up to with courage. Half-hearted reforms will not break it down; only vigorous, positive and original initiatives will win through.

As Chairman of Bulmers, the world's largest cider-makers, I am naturally proud that our productivity increases in some recent years have been about ten times the national average ($21\frac{1}{2}$ per cent in 1975–6). We have taken the initiative in a number of unusual ways. Some eight years ago, to emphasise that our shopfloor workers were regarded just as highly as our office workers, we discontinued the practice of clocking on and off. Foremen are now responsible for seeing that their people arrive on the job punctually, and the new team spirit which has developed has led to a situation in which time-keeping has actually improved.

A more flamboyant initiative, but one which others may be less inclined to follow is that I, the Chairman of the company, and some of the other directors, spend whole days working at a shopfloor task—with the support of the unions, incidentally—a day on the production line in some relatively unskilled position, or a day on the delivery lorries, acting as a driver's mate.

These instances are quoted only to illustrate the type of relatively simple initiatives which I claim can produce far more than proportionate response. Many executives, hardened to big company conditions, find it impossible to conceive that such initiatives can be either practical or rewarding, but, in fact, I know that, in my own company and elsewhere, they have worked and have produced outstanding improvements in industrial relations. They have also helped, incidentally, to give the executive a healthy sense of proportion!

In Bulmers, not a single hour's production has been lost through any form of industrial dispute for eight years. This record may be seen by many as convincing evidence that a new approach, a really personal approach, can produce results which are beneficial to workers and shareholders alike.

7
LEADERS MUST HAVE OBJECTIVES

It may seem absurd to observe that leaders must know in which direction they are leading, but it is necessary to establish the principle. They must have clearly defined objectives and the climate in which these are determined is highly significant. In Britain today, the objective-setting climate is something less than favourable and this is due, in part, to an irrational respect for tradition, an inevitable characteristic perhaps in an ageing individual, but one which ought not to be allowed to influence society, the future hope for which lies in its ability to renew itself.

Recorded history in Britain dates back for a thousand years and, quite naturally, tradition there is of greater significance than in newer societies, like those of the United States or Australia. Respect for tradition in this country is instinctive and is a very potent factor in our thinking. Whilst reform is always suspect, tradition has an appealing quality of respectability, with the result that, in a society which has a strong resistance to change, people who want to do things differently are rarely regarded with much favour.

This attitude is not peculiar to conservatives although perhaps the Conservative Party is rather more to blame for its consequences, since they have endorsed it more publicly and for a very long time. The Labour Party, in its own way, worships just as many sacred cows, although cows of a somewhat different breed. The issue of nationalisation, for example, is talked about as if it were of the same relative significance as in the days of the exploiting private mineowners.

Whatever our political persuasion may be, in today's

Leaders must know where they are going. (*Radio Times Hulton Picture Library*)

backs-to-the-wall situation we should unite in preventing the scapegoats of yesterday from serving as irrelevant issues in arguments about the problems of today.

The merit of tradition, for which we have such an ingrained respect, must be assessed in contemporary perspective, especially when it impinges upon our economic activity. What we did yesterday may have been based on well tried principles and could, at that time, have worked satisfactorily, but whether it is good today depends very much upon today's environment, for it is a characteristic of today's society that the pace of change is forever accelerating. In this situation, our response to reform must be progressively more effective.

> '*The only living organisms which survive are those which adapt themselves to change.*'
>
> *Field Marshal Slim*

The situation in which British industry finds itself, as a consequence of this inherent resistance to change, is now so serious that one can predict, with some confidence, a reversal of society's attitude: in fact, it is safe to say that better results would almost certainly follow if tradition became suspect and reform became respectable. When would-be innovators are encouraged, by a change in the prevailing climate, to bring forward their ideas, then, at least, constructive discussions on their merit can take place and up-to-date objectives are more likely to be determined and even implemented.

At present, many public and private enterprises either have no defined objectives at all, or are working to objectives which have long been obsolete, but tradition often ensures that out-dated objectives become part of the very fabric of an organisation. Objectives which have been sanctified by years of unquestioning acceptance do not even get on today's agenda for discussion.

> *'If the trumpet give an uncertain sound, who shall prepare himself to the battle)'*
>
> *St Paul to the Corinthians*

Fifty years ago, in our cider works, for example, the entire output was despatched in wooden barrels which needed to be emptied within three months of filling. In consequence, the firm's warehouse applied rigid principles of stock control on the basis of first in, first out. Sales demand and production methods changed imperceptibly over half a century and eventually only 15 per cent of the product was being despatched in the wood, the rest being in bottles and consequently staying in good condition indefinitely. However, the principles of first in, first out were still applied to the bottled stock, with six clerks assiduously maintaining the necessary records, and vehicles being loaded accordingly. When this principle was finally questioned and the practice abandoned, five of the clerks became supernumerary and could be used in more profitable ways, whilst the throughput of the warehouse increased by 32 per cent overnight. Such instances are not uncommon in British industry.

31

The crystallisation of outdated objectives is frequently the cause of death, not only of individual firms, but also, in some cases, of entire industries, especially those situated in traditional product areas. Where now is the leadership of the world's stainless steel industry which was once the glory of Sheffield? What has become of the textile supremacy of Lancashire and Yorkshire, or the paramount position of the Midlands motor cycle industry? All have been superseded by the innovations of foreigners, thanks to the complacent acceptance, by top managers, of hallowed traditions.

If Britain's economic decline is to be reversed, archaic industrial beliefs must be firmly set aside. Courageous personal leadership from the very top must develop a new environment in which the spirited initiative of individuals is not only tolerated, but actively encouraged. Neither the exaggerated caution of the technocrat, nor the cold rationality of the specialist must be allowed to kill the entrepreneurial initiative so sorely needed by British industry. Executives who display a morbid interest in the preservation of the *status quo* must be replaced by those more far-sighted and with a greater flexibility of mind. Only then will a climate be created in which new objectives can be initiated which are truly relevant to the needs of the time.

8

A SUITABLE FRAMEWORK
FOR LEADERSHIP

For personal leadership to be able to demonstrate the proven advantages of the whole-team approach, there must exist a simple and clearly defined structure of organisation within which it can work. Such a structure can be likened to the chassis of the industrial car, within which management science might well be compared to the engine. Leadership will then be seen as the fuel which gives life to the engine and makes the car the vehicle for productive effort.

Consideration of the question of simplicity in an organisation structure requires, firstly, a clear understanding of the two alternative designs upon which an organisation can be based. In most organisations, what I would describe as the 'direct management structure' is most applicable, but, in large indivisible businesses, such as an oil refinery, it could be that a structure based on functional responsibility is more appropriate. The direct structure is one which is concerned to define a chain of command from top to bottom, each position being responsible for the achievement of measurable objectives. In some cases, profit accountability by product groupings may be most suitable, while, in others, responsibility according to geographical areas may provide the only practical solution. Whatever type of objective is chosen, however, the chain of command descends from, say, group managing director to product division managing director, to works manager, to departmental manager and so on, each executive being clearly and solely responsible to the one above.

A functional structure, on the other hand, is one which is divided from top to bottom between specialist activities. The chief executive might have, reporting to him, a sales director, a production director, a distribution director and so forth, and everybody in the business would answer to one of these. This pyramidal structure will be based on the nature of the activity, rather than upon such factors as profit accountability by product grouping or area.

Whichever type of structure is adopted, however, and personally I greatly prefer the direct structure, it is absolutely vital not to establish both at once and then expect the organisation still to operate effectively. In many of Britain's larger companies today, and to a similar extent in the public service, woolly thinking has allowed both structures to develop simultaneously, as a consequence of which, executive frustration is rife and there is general confusion as to *who* is the master and a corresponding reluctance to exercise authority at any level.

A standard complaint from line managers everywhere in British companies and public bodies, is that they have no authority and that there is constant interference from headquarters, or from functional executives who are not obliged to achieve tangible results. All too often, the direct line manager is *said* to be responsible, but, in the event, he is unable to discharge his obligation properly because he is not entitled to engage or discharge employees without the permission of the central personnel department, or because he cannot initiate expenditure without the concurrence of some central budgetary control unit.

It is valuable, here, to exemplify the effect which the direct structure has upon the definition of responsibility and, thus, the elimination of ambiguity as to who is responsible to whom, and for what. In a company with a direct structure and in which there is, say, a sub-division for manufacturing confectionery, the managing director of this division would have, under his direct control, not only a works manager and a sales manager, but also a chief accountant who would not be answerable to a finance director at group headquarters. Whilst the finance director at the group level might retain an element of functional control, this would enable him to define *how* to do something rather than *what* should be done. Direct orders to the divisional chief accountant would come only from his immediate divisional managing director.

34

The effect of this straightforward structure is that the people employed by the local unit come to regard their managing director as totally responsible. It will be manifest that he has, under his control, all the executives necessary to achieve the divisional objectives. Functional control from group headquarters must be minimised if the authority of the local executive is to be underwritten. It is the death of initiative, if the feeling builds up in the local unit that the only man who really matters is some remote group headquarters tycoon who presides godlike, mysterious and omniscient over the entire organisation.

The delegation of authority is more often preached than practised, but it is the hallmark of the really effective top executive. To part with authority is to part with a little of oneself, but the initiative must be taken if the longterm success of a large enterprise is to be assured. Full delegation cannot exist unless an executive has the power to select, appoint and subsequently appraise his staff, and to authorise expenditure related to his own responsibility.

Budgetary control was developed originally for the very purpose of ensuring that effective authority could be delegated. It was designed to define, and thus to enlarge, the scope of personal authority. It was intended to define liberty, rather than to promote restriction. But, today, many bureaucrats have lost sight of this, its true justification.

Budgetary control thus is a means of quantifying executive accountability. All executives should be able to say,

> I know what my objectives are, I know what my position is in the structure, I know for what I am responsible, I know to whom I answer and I only have one boss, and I know the extent of my authority and am satisfied that it is sufficient. Being clear on all these matters, I know finally that I am obliged to account for my actions, but I am happy to do so because I have confidence that they will let me get on with the job in my own way.

Management science has thus several clearly defined roles which, properly fulfilled, will allow the full resources of personal leadership to be thoroughly exploited and the personal qualities of the executive's leadership to be given free rein.

Management science is often used to define objectives, organisation structures and the responsibilities of executives, but, in practice, unfortunately, it is rarely used to institute effective systems of delegated authority. The establishment of a liberal budgetary framework is essential if the manager is to manage effectively and his employees are to benefit from his talent as a leader.

9

THE QUALITIES OF A LEADER

Previous chapters have reviewed the environment in which leadership can operate and it is now appropriate to attempt to define, in some detail, the nature of this 'personal leadership' quality. Firstly, however, it may be useful to make one more preliminary observation, one which will summarise the central justification of this quality.

The reasoning goes something like this: leadership is very much a personal quality; all persons are different, therefore, the mode of leadership cannot be standardised; each individual leader must have his own individual style which may, or may not, work, according to whether he is an effective or ineffective leader. The exercise of an individual style obviously demands an environment of freedom since, plainly, an executive cannot do things in his own way if he is constrained by a strait jacket of formalised procedure. Frontline leadership, therefore, is something which requires not only a properly structured industrial environment in which to work, but also one in which there is a high degree of freedom.

Leadership is not an exact science, but a quality peculiar to each individual who exercises it. In consequence, it is difficult to give any but the broadest definitions. 'Leadership is the art of getting things done through other people' is a popular definition, but one with which I am not entirely happy since it does not imply that the leader is a part of the team. It has also been said that 'a leader is a man who knows where he is going and can persuade other people to go with him'. I prefer this since it makes clear that there is a team and that it has a known objective. To fill in some of

the detail embraced by these broad definitions, it will be useful to define some of the particular qualities by which such leaders may be recognised.

> *'A leader is best when people barely know that he exists, not so good when people obey and acclaim him, worst when they despise him: Fail to honour people, they fail to honour you: but of a good leader, who talks little, when his work is done, his aim fulfilled, they will all say, "We did this ourselves".'*
>
> Lao Tze, c 600 BC

At the risk of stating the obvious, it must be said at once that a leader is, above all, a man who can be recognised as such, somebody who is distinctive and stands out from the crowd. If he were 7ft tall he would be instantly identifiable in a crowd, but, since few of us have unique physical qualities, it is more often the case that a leader is recognised by his nature and character.

A degree of flamboyance is not only permissible, but may even be desirable if recognition of the leader is to be made easy. Unfortunately, the toleration of personal idiosyncracy is not a quality for which British companies are well known and if subordinate leaders are to be allowed, or even encouraged, to develop qualities which will help to identify them, then the top man might well deliberately develop a few idiosyncratic activities of his own which may serve to promote a more permissive environment for his subordinates. In my own case, a desire to lead has not been the sole reason for developing my interests in motorcycling or free-fall parachuting; fortunately, I enjoy doing these things for their own sake as well.

The failure of the organisation to tolerate individuality is a barrier, the significance of which is totally underestimated. It is one which must be deliberately broken down by the man at the top. It is of little use enjoining subordinates to 'do their own thing' if the 'atmosphere' in an organisation does not permit this to occur. The problem of British industry today is not that there is a shortage of leaders, there are plenty lost in the business

(facing page) Mrs Emmeline Pankhurst, a leader recognisable as much by her actions as by her appearance. (*Radio Times Hulton Picture Library*)

undergrowth from which the environment does not encourage them to emerge.

> *'It is the adventurous who accomplish great things.'*
> *Montesquieu*

I always decline to discuss the frequently asked question of whether leaders are born or made. The question is neither here nor there if it is accepted that there are plenty waiting to be discovered. What is it that prevents their proper exploitation? First, the value of personal leadership as a vital ingredient in the improvement of productivity is simply not recognised and, second, on the rare occasions that it is, the environment of the average large enterprise does not encourage the exercise of this individual talent.

My endeavours are directed to remedying the first and most important of these problems, as, in any case, there are many notable exceptions to the second situation. Firms like GKN Ltd, for example, a large and successful group in heavy industry, with many decentralised companies which have local autonomy and in which there is ample scope for the exercise of leadership by individual executives. In firms like this, results often speak for themselves. Good sales, good productivity, good profits and a situation in which good industrial relations generally prevail.

The first leadership 'quality', then, is this ability to be recognised and the next, in order of importance, is for leaders to be able to build up, and then hold together, an effective team and a happy team. To achieve this, it is axiomatic that they must be well known as individuals, respected and accepted by the people immediately answerable to them. This is a situation which can only be developed if the leader sets out deliberately to know his team-members on a truly personal basis. It is a great mistake to believe that the relationships within a business team should be confined to matters relating only to the business activity.

(*facing page*) The epitome of twentieth-century leadership. Sir Winston Churchill appealed to the emotion rather than to the reason of the nation. (*Radio Times Hulton Picture Library*)

> *'Time spent on the personal touch is never wasted—do not stint it.'*
> *Sir Charles Morris*

The establishment of close personal relationships is essential if the quality of leadership is to express itself effectively and a leader must, therefore, develop a really genuine, but discreet, interest in the domestic background, personal interests, problems and fears, ambitions and successes of each member of his team. This is partly a question of communication, an area of great importance

Leadership is a very personal quality as Sir Malcolm Sargent shows. (*Popperfoto*)

which is discussed later, together with the initiatives which must be taken by top executives wishing to introduce a new approach to leadership within their organisations.

The third quality a leader must possess is the ability to be decisive and, since timing is often crucial, also the courage to make decisions at the right time. A leader must not postpone the making of decisions, since, in the majority of instances, it is better to make an immediate decision based upon 90 per cent information, than to make *too late* a decision based upon 100 per cent information. We are on a conveyor belt of change and if decisions are not taken when they should be taken, the chance is missed.

All too often the formation of committees and the institution of research projects are merely a means of avoiding the real responsibility of leadership, of postponing the day of decision and the announcement of unpleasant news at the very time it may be needed most. Committees have their uses, of course, for sorting out the pros and cons of a given project, but, if they are allowed to become standing committees, they will often develop a life of their own which it is subsequently almost impossible to extinguish. It is always worth remembering the saying that 'A camel is a horse designed by a committee'.

> *'There is always a strong case for doing nothing, especially for doing nothing yourself.'*
>
> *Sir Winston Churchill*

At a time of crisis, one does not form a committee, one looks to a leader.

Decisions when taken need, of course, to be right. A leader has to be a seeker after the truth and we have already touched upon this when considering the tendency of tradition to conceal the truth through prejudice, or longstanding, but mistaken, belief. Confucius is reputed to have said that it is false economy to go to bed early to save the candle if the consequence is twins.

Whilst one aspect in his sincere search for the truth is the leader's need for a sound sense of proportion, another is the necessity also to distinguish between strategy and tactics, the

43

latter decisions being those which may not always seem consistent with the broad objectives, but which may be necessary in order to attain intermediate stages.

The attainment of ultimate objectives may often involve changes in established practice or procedure and the leader must have the courage to help these changes on their way and to persuade others of their virtue. Once they have been pushed through, however, the leader must take positive steps to restore the feeling of security which is so essential if the team is to feel contented and confident. Confidence is a quality promoted more by the leader than by anybody else. If he is certain in his own ability to lead, and this certainty can be developed by training and experience, then he will generate the confidence in the team that is so vital to success. He is more likely to achieve this through diffidence, than through earnestness, and, if he goes wrong, he should exhibit not the slightest hesitation in publicly admitting his error.

The quality of being able and willing to admit that one is wrong, sometimes completely and hopelessly wrong, is so highly valued in establishing a united team spirit, that it almost pays to find errors which one can conveniently commit.

The importance also of sustaining, in the team, a healthy interest in all that may concern it, cannot be underestimated. Said the poet:

> In works of labour or of skill,
> I should be busy too,
> For Satan finds some mischief still,
> For idle hands to do.

In my experience he also generally finds mischief for idle minds.

It was said of one particular leader during the last war that his men followed him not because of his brilliant personal qualities, but rather because they could not bear to miss his next crazy but inspired undertaking. It pays enormous dividends for the leader to have something going on which maintains a certain element of surprise in his team's day-to-day activities and which promises an

(*facing page*) To maintain enthusiasm a company needs always to have something on the go. Bulmers cider train hauled by the Great Western Railway locomotive King George V emerging from the Severn Tunnel. (*HP Bulmer Ltd*)

44

element of excitement, adventure and, if possible, amusement.

Above all, it is vital to build up a consistent atmosphere of achievement and a feeling of genuine success. A very satisfying feature of all teamwork is that, once success has been achieved, it has, of itself, a certain self-generating quality which bodes well for a secure future.

The existence of pay constraints, a near to permanent feature of the economic scene in recent years, poses difficult problems for the leader of any team and their continued existence means that some of those things which previously motivated both the team and its leader must be re-thought. In today's pay-constrained, non-motivated situation, where the production of the goods takes second place to the division of the spoils, the industrious are lumped together with the slothful, and the employer is, perforce, obliged to say to the team which has boosted productivity, 'You have certainly earned more, but, unfortunately, the Government forbids me to pay you more.' It is in situations such as these that the good leader really comes into his own. He may not be able to hand out money, but at least he has the ability and, hopefully, the sincerity to be able to dispense praise. Praise is industry's cheapest and most under-utilised asset. There seems to be an inborn reluctance to praise subordinates, but this is a restraint which the good leader must overcome.

> *'You can buy a man's time, you can buy his effort, but when you hand over his wage packet it contains nothing for enthusiasm, for self-pride, for loyalty. These things the average man is ready to give freely in return for evidence that he personally counts, and that the job he does is appreciated.'*
> Sir Bertram Waring

It is much more commonplace for executives to find fault, but all too often this is only a means of bolstering a flagging ego. It is easier and conforms to the traditional conception of the successful, autocratic, whipcracking boss, to get up in the morning with the intention of finding fault and criticising. It is much more difficult to rise and think, 'Who can I say something nice to today?' But this is the attitude which needs to be cultivated, since praise actually encourages achievement and produces much greater results than criticism will ever do. The leader himself should, however, be prepared and able to accept criticism, and it does nobody any harm to remember that one's true reputation is that which is voiced behind one's back.

The traditional British view of what the boss should be like must be firmly debunked if the new style of personal leadership I advocate is to have a reasonable chance of success. Tradition has it that the boss should be able to do everybody's job better than they can themselves. But if each employee is to have pride in his own work, this is scarcely sound psychology, in fact it is almost a sure way to disruption, discontent and a reinforcement of the traditional barriers in industry which we should be trying to break down.

For example, the engineering boss should not, with easy virtuosity, demonstrate his ability to get more output from the lathe than its regular operator; on the other hand, it does no harm for him to have a try and, after a determined attempt, to find that he cannot even achieve the operator's output. It is commonly believed that, in such circumstances, the operator would promptly ask for higher wages, but, in my experience, this is by no means the response of men in organisations where a genuine team spirit has been developed.

> *'A leader is a man who has the ability to get other people to do what they don't want to do, and like it.'*
>
> *Harry Truman*

An important quality in a leader is the ability to persuade the team that they want to follow the course of action which is proposed. Lyndall Urwick, a man whom the nation ought, long ago, to have recognised for his pioneering role in progressive management and leadership thinking, used to tell members of his consulting firm that there were a number of stages in the promotion of a new idea. His management consultants needed to sell the idea in such a way that it would be accepted and implemented and, in ascending order of amenability, that there were a number

47

·of possible responses from the client's staff:

'It's contrary to the laws of God.'

'It's quite impossible.'

'We tried it once and it didn't work.'

'Since we're paying the consultant, I suppose we'll have to try it.'

'It's what I've wanted to do for years but nobody would ever let me.'

The really successful consultant was the one who succeeded in obtaining the final response to his suggestion without going through the previous ones.

To sum up, the leader is the man who approaches his problems with an understanding of people's feelings and responses, with genuine sensitivity, and with the appreciation that personal leadership is a matter of humanity not science. Thus armed, he will discover that he has the ability to inspire others to greater efforts, for his appeal will be to the emotions and to the motivating responses of every human being. Warmth and understanding are vital emotional elements of leadership ability, not quantifiable, but instantly recognisable. People react positively and happily to them without, in any way, sacrificing their critical faculties. They are qualities we all possess to some degree and are a potent force which can be developed.

These, then, are the qualities of a leader, but, to apply them in a potentially hostile environment, one more thing is needed—and in full measure—courage, simple courage.

May I conclude this chapter on a somewhat personal note. A friend who has kicked me into writing this book feels strongly that something should be said about a leader's private life, but, even after a good many years in industry, one's observations are bound to be limited.

'Leadership' does need to be carefully distinguished from megalomania, preferably by the practitioner himself. One is a quality, the other a disease, but the symptoms can often be similar. The disease has accounted for more than a few marriage break ups in the top echelons of industry, for, while leaders who

(*facing page*) Companies as well as leaders need to be distinctive and recognisable. A member of the Bulmers Sky Diving team landing at Cheltenham in 1971. (*HP Bulmer Ltd*)

emerge spontaneously are sufficiently difficult to live with, leaders who are self-appointed can often be impossible.

Busy business executives are only likely to survive to a ripe old age if they have at least one active alternative interest, the equivalent of Churchill's bricklaying, or Edward Heath's music. If they are to become really *good* leaders they should also acquire the saving grace of a strong sense of humour and, even better, an ability to appreciate the ridiculous.

It goes without saying that, if they are to overcome the pressures of office, they must take good care of their physical condition, their diet and their working habits. Above all, they must avoid total dedication to the job.

10
TELLING AND LEADING

A major factor which must be considered if the benefits of leadership are to be given full rein in an organisation, is the existence of a good communications system, from top to bottom and across, and this is an area where a pinch of good practice is worth a pound of theory. Good communications build up confidence.

Communication between two human beings is much more a matter of atmosphere and emotional relationship than of word use or applied science. Although a middle-level executive is responsible for the quality of his communications down the line, he is often obliged to promote his own information channels with his superiors. 'Nobody ever tells me anything', is one of the most frequently heard complaints at the middle level of any enterprise. If a leader is to operate effectively, it is clear that he must be given as much information as is necessary for him to understand what his objectives are and to be secure in the confidence of the authority which has been delegated to him.

As the middle manager spends much of his time deliberating with his peers, it is obvious that, as well as communicating upwards and downwards, communications must also work effectively in a sideways direction. In so far as the people who come under his control are concerned, however, he has a much freer hand, and it should be his aim to ensure that commnications are excellent in a two-way sense. If we want to talk to other people we must also be prepared to listen to what they have to say. It is just as important for the executive to know what his subordinates are thinking as it is for them to know what he is thinking.

This is another area of management in which we have been bemused by a too scientific approach. It is a great mistake to for-

Good communications build up confidence and achieve results. (*Radio Times Hulton Picture Library*)

malise such a simple human occupation as talk. The consultative committees, so beloved of governments and industrial relations departments, are all very well in their own limited way, but they do little to ensure that Smith and Jones tell each other what they each wish and need to know. A serious regard for the personal qualities of leadership will provide more help on communication than any attempt on my part to lay down a new set of theoretical principles. It is sufficient at this point to consider only one main question which is of general applicability. 'How much information should be passed upwards and downwards?'

It is not at all easy to quantify such an indistinct element as communication, but there is a generality which can be used as a helpful guide. If the manager is to err on one side or the other, it is far, far better for him to pass *too much* information downwards than to pass *too little*. The usual argument against overwhelming the man below with information is that much of it is not properly understood, but this overlooks one vital psychological factor, the sort of factor which is the very stuff of leadership. The mere fact that the man down the line is offered more, rather than less, information promotes a feeling of confidence and of trust in his superiors. There is a universal human fear of the dark and to offer more light engenders a stronger sense of security.

At present, we certainly err on the side of passing more information than is really necessary to the shareholders, since auditors, often pedantic rather than practical, encourage directors in the average company report to cover detail with excessive zeal. But there is very little evidence to indicate that the average shareholder is more intelligent, or more discerning, than the average worker.

It is safe to assert that, in the vast majority of organisations, at present, a situation prevails under which too little information is passed down and too much information is required to be passed up.

Another general point in connection with communication concerns the quality of the information which is passed downwards. Good leadership shows up best when times are tough—it is a weak policy to pass down only the good news. The workforce—the team—should be treated as responsible people. The content of the house magazines of some large organisations appears to pass on only one message—'Look how good we all are!' This is the approach of gutless managers, endeavouring to appease the displeasure of readers who, in the final analysis, they fear. To pass bad news down the line requires courage, but then courage is almost the most essential quality of effective leadership.

Another way in which top managers often shelter the rank and file from the facts of life, is by maintaining a perpetual pretence that nothing ever goes wrong and that no mistakes are ever made. It is often said with truth, however, that the man who never made a mistake never made anything of importance. We learn much from our mistakes. One of the most commonly believed fallacies is that the admission of error undermines the authority of people at the top. In practice, the reverse is the case. In some ways, the admission of error often helps to promote confidence within a team; there is a natural human inclination to admire people who are big enough to admit that they are not always right. The admission of imperfection is the beginning of mutual respect. The perfect superior is held in far less esteem than one who admits to the occasional frailty.

All of the foregoing is based on one overriding premise: that the leader is a man of integrity; quite simply that his record promotes a feeling of trust in those whom he leads.

11

FINDING THE LEADER

Although this book is about leadership, certain areas of management which are related to it must also be reviewed. Leadership is a personal quality based upon an instinctive understanding of human relationships and the recognition of this quality in others is a factor of importance in the recruitment, selection and training of leaders.

It is the clear responsibility of a higher executive to ensure that an environment exists in which his subordinates' resources of leadership can be fully utilised. It ought also to be the responsibility of each executive to choose and recruit his own subordinates, since he will stand or fall on their performance.

On his appointment to a new post he will, of course, find other people already there—the staff he has inherited. For a time he may well take them as he finds them, but, if they do not match up to the requirements of their jobs, he may also have a duty to replace them at some point, a task which has been made extremely difficult by the recent spate of mollycoddling legislation.

In recent years, also, the vital responsibilities of recruitment and selection have been progressively whittled away from responsible executives, on the ground that this relieves them of a time-consuming task. The task has finished up in the hands of central personnel departments, or of outside recruitment firms.

An even worse state of affairs sometimes prevails in the armed services, the civil service and the nationalised industries. Here, it is often the case that responsible executives have no say at all in the appointment of their subordinates, but are obliged to make do with whoever some specialist central department chooses to post to them.

The situation prevailing in some big companies is often little better. A central department, or an external recruitment company, may provide the executives with a short list of five applicants who had responded, initially, to an advertisement worded with little or no consultation with the executive. The applicants have been subjected to a weeding-out process, dependent upon selection factors over which he has had no influence and which, all too often, have little regard for leadership quality. The executive is then expected to make his final selection, generally from applicants that the outside 'experts' believe he *ought* to want.

If one accepts the premise that one of the most significant responsibilities of any leader is the selection of his team, then it is surely iniquitous that he should be obliged by, short-sighted and

Humility can be an asset to a leader. (*HP Bulmer Ltd*)

ill-conceived procedures, to subcontract this paramount responsibility to somebody who is, thereafter, not accountable.
Apologists of these methods claim that the executive is relieved of
a great deal of tiresome work by the 'service' provided by the personnel department or the selection firm. Styles of leadership vary
a great deal from one executive to another, however, and the
criteria applied to the processes of advertisement and selection by
one person may be very different indeed from those applied by
another. In my own case, for example, I tend to rate non-conformity and innovative capacity very much more highly than the
average personnel department which, in my experience, tends to
produce nice, safe, colourless candidates whose main recommen-
dation is that they will fit neatly into the organisation and cause
little trouble.

A standard characteristic of centralised recruitment is the
stress which is placed upon 'experience'. It is really quite extraordinary how many businessmen equate the word 'experience' with
'good experience', for, in reality, there is very little justification
for doing so. Experience gained with some firms, and, in particular, old-established ones which are perhaps already on the
downward path, can be thoroughly *bad* experience.

> *'People who say they have 30 years' experience generally mean that they have one
> year's experience 30 times over.'*
> *Abraham Lincoln*

It is better to recruit a man who has had no experience at all,
but who has an open mind and shows promise, rather than risk
the importation of thoroughly bad practices into an organisation
which may not already be suffering from them. True leaders, of
course, learn by experience.

Many executives whom I have appointed to positions over the
years and who have, in the event, proved to be successful, were
ones who would almost certainly have been eliminated without
interview by some personnel selection firms, a fact which I have
established to my own satisfaction in an unusual way. During my
career I have had six different jobs, four of which I found as a

result of my own approaches. In the case of the other two, I applied to a box number for a firm of selection consultants, and also to an open advertisement for what was, in fact, the client, although, at the time, of course, I did not know this. In both cases, as a result of my direct application to the firm I was given the job and it was only later that I discovered that the box number advertisement, for which I had been turned down without interview by the consultants, was in fact the same job which I had successfully obtained.

The wording of advertisements is crucial and the ultimate message which can be conveyed is that 'we are a nice sort of firm to work for and you would enjoy being with us'. Advertisements inserted by some recruitment firms and personnel departments often verge on the pompous and can convey quite the reverse idea. Such advertisements often begin with phrases like 'a famous public company with an outstanding record of success in consumer goods is proceeding to the appointment of a . . .' and quite often in the 'quality' press we see 'prestige' advertisements of the 'forward into the future with Bloggs & Sons . . .' type. Seemingly the larger the business concern, the more admissable is corporate conceit.

My own personal view, is that a good advertisement gives the name of the employer and his location, a clear indication of the salary on offer, how the post fits into the organisation structure, its duties, and the authority to be delegated. Moreover, I much prefer that an applicant be invited to address his letter to the executive to whom he will ultimately be answerable.

I realise that these ideas may not be generally accepted and I must confess to having once greatly offended a famous captain of industry for whom I worked, by advertising for a financial controller with the phrase 'a reformed consultant will not come amiss'. The chairman did not think this was at all funny. More recently I raised 606 good applications for a managing director post by including a phrase to which over half the applicants referred in their letters, it read 'Bulmers has a distinctive and not too earnest style of management'. It definitely pays to demonstrate a degree of pleasant informality.

Some business schools seem to have a somewhat blinkered preoccupation with scientific management and this lead has been

Advertisements should convey atmosphere—as essential an ingredient as the hard facts. (*HP Bulmer Ltd*)

followed in the personnel policies of some firms. Such policies, I fear, often destroy completely much of the executive responsibility upon which a firm's success should depend.

On the other hand, there are many concerns who do understand the role of expertise, who do appreciate the distinction between direct and functional management, and the reasons why the two systems cannot operate simultaneously. These are ones who have good personnel departments which understand that their most effective role is to reinforce, not erode, the authority of direct line executives, to act in a 'staff' rather than an executive capacity, and to give sound advice and service to the direct line man.

My somewhat wild swipes at personnel departments should, therefore, not be taken to undervalue the excellent service which, in fact, many give in the field of executive recruitment, by the acknowledgement and appraisal of replies, and in the subsequent administration of interview and appointment procedures.

So much for a leader's recruitment responsibilities, and now a final few words upon training. I have already said that, in my view, Britain has no shortage of leaders, but that many are suppressed by the system, or lost in the organisational labyrinth. When they are unearthed, it should be remembered that they may need training and encouragement to revive their confidence in their leadership ability. They may need new opportunities to prove to themselves that they can initiate, form a team and achieve solid results. It will be clear from this that I am much in favour of training on the job and that I applaud the 'Action Learning' projects which Professor Reginald Revans, with the backing of Sir Arnold Weinstock and the GEC, is seeking to promote.

The Leadership Trust, which my own company initiated, is based on a similar philosophy and seeks to gain support for the whole principle of achievement through teamwork and through people.

12

THE REVIVAL OF LEADERSHIP

Since the 1950s, there has been an explosion of interest in management science and a tremendous amount of money has been spent on management education. In particular, there has been massive investment in business schools; in faculties at over thirty universities, and departments in most large polytechnics have come into being. These have been supplemented by the Manpower Services Commission, the Training Services Agency and some twenty-five training boards. To say the least, bureaucracy in management education and training is badly in need of streamlining.

Many people, including myself, are beginning to have doubts about the pay-off from this investment. I believe that much of it may have been counter-productive in that, by giving official support to the mistaken belief that management science provides the way to salvation, it has diverted attention from the much more important need for better personal leadership in industry. Management science may help, but it is only a tool, the selection and training of people with leadership qualities is the real key to solid achievement. The effective use of human resources must be given absolute priority if we are to solve our present economic crisis.

The spark of initiative, the subconscious urge in leaders to make their mark, Lord Wavell's 'irrational tenth' in the aspiring leader, are all of far greater importance than whatever happens to be the currently fashionable management science.

Near to the beginning of this book, I said that my thoughts might be seen only as a restatement of the obvious, but perhaps the obvious needs to be restated, if we are to redress the distorted

balance which has developed in recent years through our preoccupation with management science. We all must agree that
action, rather than talk, is needed now, to arrest the nation's
economic decline—how people can learn to be more effective
is the real issue. My approach is heavily slanted towards
the better utilisation of each individual's personal talents and
the merit of this approach is that it is easily and clearly understood. If applied, it can produce the quick, solid and tangible
results which have been achieved in the company for which I
work and which, to varying extents, have been recorded in other
companies which have used a similar approach. The nation's
economic situation is now so parlous that quick, simple measures
are required, rather than endless talk about ever-more
sophisticated remedies of much greater complexity.

The measures should be those which can be initiated and
implemented at unit level. Not only is it a delusion to believe
that solutions will come down from on high—from the TUC, the
CBI, NEDO, or from the Government, but it is also an evasion
of personal responsibility. The men and women who comprise
each business, each management unit, should think of themselves
as being all together in a lifeboat. They must row together as a
team in the same direction if they are to overcome the surrounding economic hazards. Leadership rather than science is required
to promote this unity of purpose. Science may promote the
logic of pulling together, but inspired leadership stands more
chance of achieving this ideal.

I make no claim that this approach is the only one; there may be
others and they may achieve results. I have found recently,
however, that a number of responsible, professional bodies are
very much more in favour of this direct and humane approach
than some of the bodies concerned with the propagation of
management science.

It is my hope that the British Institute of Management and
other national and local bodies will, in future, take a clearer
and more positive line on the constituent elements of good
management, with a much greater stress on the vital role of the
manager as a leader. Whilst many leading teaching estab-
lishments have made a copious contribution to sophisticated
management in the last twenty years or so, the value of this con-

tribution would have been greatly enhanced if the schools had concerned themselves less deeply with the tools of management and rather more with the personal performance of the manager himself. If they had found time to lay at least some stress on the significance of those vital qualities which I contend are used far too little in industry today, then the benefits of their scientific thinking might have had a greater impact on national productivity and the nation's economic achievement.

Teachers should have an objective approach to constructive suggestion, however, and I hope sincerely that those responsible for management education will consider my proposals, rather than dismiss them merely on the grounds of brash idealism or poor presentation. I claim for my philosophy that it is tangible, that it is appealing, that it proposes a definite course of action which can be quickly understood, seized upon and implemented. My philosophy is age old; I am not inventing the wheel, only attempting to revive a fundamental truth connected with human behaviour.

Plainly such a philosophy must be tailored to individual situations; but it can always be reduced to two basic elements, both of which can be made to work if the will exists at the top to promote them vigorously. The first is that an executive's own awareness of the vital significance of his leadership responsibility can be awakened and solidified.

The second element is that employers have to ensure that executives are provided with new scope within the organisation to exercise their leadership talent. This change is much more difficult to implement and requires firm and resolute initiative, and action from the very top. Unless chief executives sincerely believe in the idea, the benefits of personal leadership will never be fully realised.

Nor is it always possible to adopt the principle of management by leadership when market pressures expose the failure of the authoritarian approach. Once industrial confrontation has worked its wicked will repentance may come too late. A leader of Napoleonic stature would be required to rescue some British firms from their legacy of complacency, improvident amalgamation, internal strife and colourless management.

The time to spotlight leadership is before the trouble starts,

63

ideas like plants, grow best on weed-free soil. I have already quoted the incomparable Winston, 'There is always a case for doing nothing, especially for doing nothing yourself'. He might well have added, 'The strongest case of all is for doing nothing yourself NOW'. John Garnett of the Industrial Society, possibly Britain's most brilliant speaker on leadership, often says that an idea is of little use in practical management terms unless an executive can go to his office on the following morning and say, 'I am going to do it now'.

What then might senior executives in public and private enterprise – who have done me the honour of reading this far – do tomorrow morning? They might check that: objectives exist; the structure is clear; executives have authority; leaders are recognised; conformity is discouraged; initiative is encouraged; information flows freely; happiness is promoted; restriction is minimised; and praise is dispensed. Above all, the man at the top must take positive steps to break down those barriers within the firm which divide management and men, to replace instinctive antagonism by tolerant understanding, to encourage appeals to the heart rather than to the head.

The cynics will still assert that my ideas are starry-eyed, that they would not work at British Leyland. (Sir Herbert Austin would not have said so.) But what alternative is now on offer? Nobody will argue that we are not as a Nation in dire economic straits.

To the doubting Thomases therefore I can only say one more thing – try the leadership approach and see – it works!

'Of the many gifts which the English possess, the most engaging to my mind is their inextinguishable optimism. Whole continents may sink like Atlantis below the waves, whole empires may dissolve before their very eyes, and the English will persist in persuading themselves that all misfortune has been designed as some blessing in disguise and that it is certain to be fine on Sunday.'
Harold Nicholson